The Adventures of

BROTHER BIDDLE

by Rob Suggs

*The misguided escapades of
America's favorite cartoon preacher*

Other wonderful, fine *Door* Books:

101 Things To Do During a Dull Sermon

The Door Interviews

The Adventures of

BROTHER BIDDLE

by Rob Suggs

The Door / ZONDERVAN

The Adventures of Brother Biddle

Copyright © 1990 by Youth Specialties, Inc.
1224 Greenfield Drive, El Cajon, CA 92021.

Youth Specialties Books are copublished with
Zondervan Publishing House, 1415 Lake Drive,
S.E., Grand Rapids, MI 49506.

ISBN: 0-310-51761-3

Written, illustrated, proofread, sketched, and sold
from the trunk of his car in church parking lots
everywhere by Rob Suggs, fourth cousin to Brother
Biddle on his mother's aunt's husband's best
friend's side of the family.

Printed in the United States of America.

90 91 92 93 94 95 96 / CH / 10 9 8 7 6 5 4 3 2 1

Introduction

Mark Twain once said that there would be no humor in heaven because all humor is built on the incongruities of human existence. Maybe there is truth to what Mark Twain had to say to us, but since we are not in heaven, the kind of humor that Rob Suggs lays before us does us all a lot of good.

First of all, it does let us see the incongruities of our existence and particularly the incongruities of dear Brother Biddle. He is a man who is sincerely trying to be the prophet of God, but often is blinded to the ludicrous contradictions of his message that are part of his everyday life. Those of us who try to be prophetic as we preach the gospel need to be aware that we come across in many ways to other people, and we will all be a lot healthier if we can join in the laughter that is directed at all of us.

Brother Biddle is also one of those preachers who is trying to be relevant. Once again, none of us are about to fall hip to that, but at the same time we are made to see how easily we are seduced into stupid fads that deserve to be mocked.

Of course, one of the funniest things may be this introduction. Academic sociologists like me always have to see some profound meaning in the stuff like Brother Biddle. Why can't we just stand back and see these strips for what they are—a lot of fun? What Biddle does for me when I really get down to it is that it not only gets me to laugh at myself, but lets me laugh at a lot of things that are going on in church ministry. Once I see how funny they are in Brother Biddle's life, they become funny when I see them in my own. That makes my life a lot more enjoyable. What else can one ask of a good Christian book?

Yours with tongue in cheek,

Tony Campolo
Professor of Sociology
Eastern College

WE MIGHT AS WELL GET THIS BOOK ROLLING, YOU GUYS... WE'VE GOT ELEVEN YEARS TO COVER. MR. SUGGS, TELL US A LITTLE ABOUT THESE EARLY STRIPS WE'RE ABOUT TO SEE, FROM 1978.

WELL, OF COURSE I WAS A YOUNG SEMINARY STUDENT AND I WANTED TO COME UP WITH A FUNNY MINISTERIAL GUY I COULD DRAW...

SO I THOUGHT OF AN INNOCUOUS NAME... "**BIDDLE**"... SOUNDS LIKE "TWADDLE" OR "BUMBLE."

AND OF COURSE I MADE HIM **BALD**, BESPECTACLED, **CHUBBY**, AND KLUTZY... A LITURGICAL LOSER.

BUT PART OF HIS APPEAL IS HE MAKES ANY **REAL** PASTOR SEEM EXCITING. I MEAN, CAN **YOU** IMAGINE A LESS INSPIRING...

CAN WE GET **ON WITH IT?**

BUT... YOU **CAN'T** CANCEL OUR SERVICES FROM YOUR STATION! WE **TAILORED** THEM FOR OUR TELEVISION AUDIENCE!

THAT'S JUST THE POINT. THEY WERE COMING OFF OVERDONE!

WELL... I **ADMIT** IT'S HARD NOT TO BE CONSCIOUS OF THE CAMERA... BUT OUR SERVICES ARE FULL OF MEANING AND CARING! **WE CAN MINISTER TO THIS COMMUNITY!**

I'M SORRY, REV. BIDDLE.

CLICK!

IT WAS THE CHEERLEADERS. I KNOW IT WAS THE CHEERLEADERS.

TRUE DISCIPLESHIP DEMANDS **PERSONAL SPIRITUAL GROWTH!**

PREACH IT, BROTHER BIDDLE!

AMEN!

AND PERSONAL SPIRITUAL GROWTH DEMANDS **LOVE FOR THE CHURCH!**

PREACH IT, BROTHER BIDDLE!

AMEN!

AND LOVE FOR THE CHURCH DEMANDS **OBEDIENCE TO YOUR PASTOR!**

PREACH IT, BROTHER BIDDLE!

AMEN!

AND YOUR PASTOR DEMANDS **A REASONABLE SALARY INCREASE AND A LATER MODEL BUICK!**

FORGET IT, BROTHER BIDDLE!

RATS.

AMEN!

THE RAPTURE IS A SUBJECT ABOUT WHICH WE SHOULD...WELL...**CLEAR THE AIR.**

HA! WELL PUT. MY SERMON WAS ENTITLED, "PIE IN THE SKY BY AND BY: THE RAPTURE GETS ITS JUST DESSERTS."

OBVIOUSLY YOU HAVE A LOT TO SAY ABOUT THIS DOCTRINE.

NOT REALLY. I JUST LIKED THE TITLE.

WHAT ABOUT IT, BIDDLE...ARE WE LIVING IN THE END TIMES?

WELL, LET'S SEE... THIS YEAR, DIVIDED BY THE NUMBER OF HAL LINDSEY BEST SELLERS...CARRY THE 144...SUBTRACT THE TOTAL OF FALSE ALARMS IN THIS DECADE...

COULD THE ANSWER BE: "**NO ONE** KNOWS THE DAY OR THE HOUR?"

WE HAVE TO EARN OUR WINGS **EVERY** DAY...

WELCOME TO "RAPTURE EMPHASIS WEEK"! AS YOU KNOW, THE RAPTURE WILL INVOLVE ALL BELIEVERS...

JUST WHEN WE LEAST EXPECT IT WE'LL BE TAKEN INTO THE SKY! IT COULD HAPPEN **SUDDENLY** AT ANY...

SWISH!

JUST KIDDING!

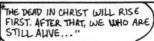

BROTHER BIDDLE, WE UNDERSTAND THE CATHOLIC/PROTESTANT SOFTBALL GAME DIDN'T WORK OUT. HAVE ECUMENICAL RELATIONS DETERIORATED?

NO... BUT ATHLETICS ARE DEFINITELY NOT THE ANSWER.

COULD YOU EXPLAIN?

ONE OF OUR GUYS SPIKED THEIR SHORTSTOP AND SAID: "**THAT** WAS FOR THE SPANISH INQUISITION."

WHAT A SHAME WE CAN'T BE **ONE CHURCH.**

NOT REALLY; **BASEBALL** HAS TWO LEAGUES. ONE DAY WE'LL HAVE A THEOLOGICAL WORLD SERIES IN HEAVEN: CALVIN PITCHING, WESLEY AT SHORT, LUTHER BEHIND THE PLATE. MAYBE AQUINAS PLAYING THIRD...

HOW ABOUT SOME OF THE MODERN THEOLOGIANS?

OUT IN LEFT FIELD.

...AND ONE MORE ANNOUNCEMENT: I HOPE YOU'LL ALL BE WITH US THIS AFTERNOON FOR CHURCH SOFTBALL!

IT'LL BE A REAL GRUDGE MATCH AGAINST A RIVAL CHURCH, SAINT EUGENE OF THE CROSS, FROM DOWN THE BLOCK!

SO COME ON OUT WITH A SPIRIT OF FINE FELLOWSHIP AND SUPPORT YOUR CHURCH!

First Church

TODAY IN SOFTBALL
REFORMATION II
CATHOLICS VS. PROTESTANTS
FIRST CHURCH VS ST. EUGENE OF THE CROSS

WELL, HERE COME YOUR TWO MISADVENTURES WITH TELEVANGELISTS. MUST WE ENDURE ANOTHER SHOT AT THESE GUYS?

WELL, YOU HAVE TO KEEP IN MIND THIS IS **HISTORY**. THESE STORIES HAPPENED **YEARS** BEFORE THE BIG SCANDALS.

WHAT CAN WE LEARN FROM THE ELECTRONIC CHURCH?

POWER CORRUPTS. ABSOLUTE POWER CORRUPTS ABSOLUTELY.

EVERYONE SHOULD HAVE SOMEONE TO WHOM THEY'RE **ACCOUNTABLE!**

AH. SINCE YOU BROUGHT IT UP... TO WHOM AM **I** ACCOUNTABLE? LET'S JUST SAY THAT SUGGS FORESAW THESE DANGERS AND BUILT IN SOME CHECKS AND BALANCES.

WHAT KIND OF CHECKS AND B

WHO ARE YOU TALKING TO IN HERE, SONNY BOY? NOT DOING YER **BOOK** ON CHURCH TIME, ARE YA? PAID FOR BY **MY** TITHES AND OFFERINGS?

I'M SORRY, BROTHER BIDDLE ISN'T TAKING ANY CALLS. HE SPENDS THIS TIME ALONE EVERY DAY.

IT'S THE "PAY THE LORD CLUB" WITH JIM AND TAMMY FAYE FAKKER!

HEE HEE! TASTE DEATH, FAKKER!

THWUK! THWUK! THWUK!

BROTHER BIDDLE, I **WISH** YOU'D KEEP THAT TURNED DOWN.

SLAM!

OFF MY CASE, MS. WADDLE! I'M HAVING MY QUIET TIME!

MY FIRST GUEST IS A BORN-AGAIN AXE-MURDERER WHO...

NO OFFENSE TO YOUR MINISTRY, BIDDLE, BUT WE GOTTA THINK **BIG!** WE'RE TALKING **CANCER** HERE! THE BIG C!

ANYWAY, JESUS HAS COMMANDED IT! HE'S SUGGESTED SPECIFIC FINANCIAL ARRANGEMENTS... BESIDES—WHAT CAN ONE SMALL CHURCH LIKE **YOURS** DO?

SUPPORT **ONE** MISSIONARY WHO **NEEDS** US.

JESUS SAYS HE READ IN "READER'S DIGEST" THE COMMIES ARE GETTING ALL THAT.

WELL, TELL JESUS NOT TO BELIEVE EVERYTHING HE READS!

...AND HE SAID, "WHEN ARE YOU AND YOUR FOLLOWERS GOING TO START OBEYING ME? WHEN??"

AND HE JUST ABOUT KICKED OVER MY PRAYER TOWER IN HIS ANXIETY! IF YOU COULD JUST HAVE BEEN THERE ALL YOUR PEOPLE WOULD GIVE THEIR $240.00 GLADLY!

FLORAL MEMORIAL HOSPITAL

THEY PROBABLY WILL ANYWAY... BUT TELL ME: AFTER CANCER BITES THE DUST, WHERE DOES JESUS GO FROM HERE?

WHO KNOWS, BIDDLE? ACNE; ASTHMA; MAYBE EVEN HERPES! THE LORD MOVES IN MYSTERIOUS WAYS!

REALLY.

WE HAD NO IDEA JOB SECURITY WAS SUCH A TENSE ISSUE FOR MINISTERIAL FOLK.

TELL ME ABOUT IT... I KNEW I WAS IN TROUBLE WHEN THEY INSTALLED A REVOLVING DOOR IN MY OFFICE...

DO YOU EVER FEEL DISCARDED LIKE ANOTHER PIECE OF SANCTUARY FURNITURE?

ARE YOU KIDDING? THEY HATE CHANGING THE FURNITURE, OR THE ORDER OF WORSHIP, OR THE HYMNS, OR THE CARPET, OR THE ATTENDANCE, OR...

YOU GAIN SOME POSITIVES FROM MOVING AROUND, DON'T YOU? WISDOM, A SENSE OF URGENCY OF YOUR MESSAGE...

YEAH, BUT ESPECIALLY THE FREQUENT MOVER POINTS ON OUR VAN LINE!

MINISTERS WERE NEVER MEANT TO DO ALL THE WORK!

IN THE CHURCH WE'RE ALL PART OF A TEAM... I'M JUST THE QUARTERBACK!

TREAT ME JUST LIKE ANY OTHER MEMBER OF A TEAM...

I CAN'T BELIEVE THEY TRADED ME TO THIRD CHURCH FOR A YOUTH DIRECTOR, TWO CUSTODIANS AND A DEACON TO BE NAMED LATER!

MORE DEMANDS.... "ALL THE MEN HAVE TO DRESS IN TIGHTS AND DO AEROBICS WITH US..."

"THE ABOLITION OF MEN'S SOFTBALL TO BE REPLACED BY SEWING AND CAKE-DECORATING LEAGUES??"

"...PAINT THE STEEPLE **PINK?**" MISS NAOMI, THIS **CAN'T** GET WORSE...

DON'T BLOW THE CHANCE TO STAY AS MY **ASSISTANT** PASTOR.

IT CAN GET WORSE.

HONEY, YOU'LL NEVER BELIEVE... WAIT, HOLD ON A SECOND...

BROTHER BIDDLE, THE EMPIRE HAS STRUCK **BACK!**

THE MEN'S BIBLE CLASS FORMED A MALE GUERRILLA COUNTERFORCE AND WE'VE **CRUSHED THE REBELLION!**

IT GOT NASTY BUT MOST OF THEM FELL APART WHEN WE THREATENED TO STOP MOWING OUR LAWNS.

ANYHOW, WE HAD TO BLOW UP THE NEW GYM TO STIFLE THE LADIES' JAZZERCIZE MOB...

HELLO, I'M DAN RATHER, ANYBODY HOME?

Honey, I may be late....

A RECENT STUDY INDICATES PEOPLE ARE ATTENDING CHURCH MORE BUT GIVING LESS.

I KNOW... I HOPE THEY'RE GOING TO ENJOY WORSHIPPING IN THE DARK.

SO TITHING IS A HARD SELL THESE DAYS?

THE CONSUMER IN THE PEW IS A TOUGH NUT TO CRACK. OUR CHURCH IS FULL OF TOUGH NUTS, AS A MATTER OF FACT.

IS THE CHURCH SHIFTING TO SOPHISTICATED, SECULAR MODELS FOR FUND-RAISING?

I'M NOT SURE. I'LL ASK OUR FINANCIAL CONSULTANT.

HENRY...FIRST CHURCH IS FUND-RAISING AGAIN.

OH?

I HAVEN'T SEEN THE USUAL LETTER FROM BROTHER BIDDLE.

NEITHER HAVE I...

I THINK HE'S PROMOTING THROUGH THE SUNDAY SCHOOL THIS YEAR!

TITHE TILL IT HURTS

BEAT THIRD CHURCH

WOULD YOU GYP ME?

...AND I'D LIKE TO CHALLENGE EVERYBODY ON THE BOWLING TEAM TO PLEDGE **$1.25** LIKE ME! I'LL BRING IT TO CHURCH NEXT EASTER!

GEE, THANKS!

KEEP THOSE CALLS COMING IN, FOLKS! ONLY NINE THOUSAND NINE HUNDRED SEVENTY-EIGHT DOLLARS TO GO!

$21.87

L:$10,000

AH...THIS **COULD** BE THE BIG ONE!

RING!

THIS IS THE PHONE COMPANY. WE'D LIKE TO CHALLENGE YOU TO PAY YOUR BILL OF $27.94 OR WE'LL CUT YOU OFF.

$60

GOAL: $10,000

DING DING DING!

THAT MUST HAVE BEEN THE FIRST TELETHON **EVER** TO FINISH IN THE RED.

I'VE TRIED TEE SHIRTS AND BALLOONS. I BEGGED FROM THE PULPIT. I STAGED A TELETHON.

SO I GUESS IT'S BACK TO **TRADITIONAL** FUND-RAISING...

I HATE AIRPORTS.

OH, GEE, A REVERSE MOHAWK. I WANNA BE IN **YOUR** CULT!

FIRST CHURCH

Suggs

Brother Biddle

by Rob Suggs

Panel 2: BROTHER BIDDLE? THAT NEWS WRITER IS HERE TO SEE YOU.

FINE! SEND HIM RIGHT IN!

Panel 3: I'M HERE TO DO THE USUAL PIECE ON RELIGIOUS TRENDS, BROTHER BEATLE.

IT'S **BIDDLE**, ACTUALLY. PULL UP A CHAIR!

Panel 4: I'M **NEW** ON THE GOD BEAT, YA KNOW! I USUALLY COVER THE **POLITICAL** TURF. YA MIGHT CALL ME A "RELIGIOUS-RAP ROOKIE!"

"GOD BEAT?"

Panel 5: NOW I JUST HAVE A FEW QUESTIONS... FATHER FIDDLE, HOW DO YOU SEE THE CHURCH OF 1984?

WELL, FIRST, I'M JUST **BROTHER** BIDDLE. I ANSWER TO "FATHER" ONLY AT HOME, HA HA.

I SEE...

Panel 6: "At First Church, Rev. Biddle discards traditional religious concepts, feeling these should be left at home."

Panel 7: NOW TO ANSWER YOUR QUESTION, WITH THE DIVERSITY WE HAVE TODAY, I'D BE PRESUMPTUOUS TO TRY TO SPEAK FOR A WHOLE **DENOMINATION**, MUCH LESS THE CHRISTIAN FAITH AS A WHOLE!

SEE HERE, SLUDGE! I, **BROTHER BIDDLE, DEMAND** TO KNOW WHAT ASPERSIONS YOU CAST UPON MY NAME!

JUST THAT YOU'RE A LEFTIST, ATHEISTIC TWIT DESTINED FOR THE DEITY'S DUMPSTER OF DESTRUCTION.

ON WHAT GROUNDS?

THIS HERE ARTICLE QUOTES YOU AS SAYIN' THE **BIBLE** IS **"HARD TO SWALLOW"** AND **"FOR PEOPLE WHO ARE DESPERATE."**

A **MISQUOTE!** I **ACTUALLY** SAID THE BIBLE IS SOMETHING WE SHOULD **"STRUGGLE TO DIGEST"**... AND THAT **"PEOPLE ARE DESPERATE FOR"** IT. CHECK YOUR **SOURCES,** BUSTER!

TUT, TUT. I'M NOT **PERFECT,** ONLY FORGIVEN. **NEXT!**

NOT SO FAST! I DEMAND THAT YOU **CLEAR MY NAME!**

MAYBE... JUST TELL ME: ARE YOU A PRO-LIFE, PRAYERINSCHOOL, PLENARYVERBAL, PRE-MILLENNIAL PREDESTINARY **PREVANGELICAL...** OR A **LIB'RAL??**

SLUDGE... ARE THOSE YOUR **ONLY** TWO CHOICES?

SELECT **ONE!**

NOPE. YOU KEEP YOUR MULTIPLE-CHOICE DOCTRINE, AND I'LL KEEP MY ESSAY-QUESTION FAITH.

COMMIE.

OO! MY POP JUST GAVE YOU A METAPHOR-WHIPPING, MISTER!

Brother Biddle

NON-WHITES PLEASE MOVE TO THE REAR OF THE PULPIT

by Rob Suggs

WELCOME TO "NON-WHITE AWARENESS WEEK," A DELIGHTFUL TIME OF GUILT-GRAPPLING AND CONSCIENCE-PUMMELING WE LOOK FORWARD TO EVERY YEAR!

LET'S KICK OFF THIS MORNING'S SET WITH A BROTHER OF THE NON-WHITE PERSUASION! HE'S BLACK, HE'S ANGRY AND HE'S KAREEM ABDUL WESLEY OF THE IRRITATED NEGRO FELLOWSHIP!

'MORNING, HONKIES!

FIRST LET ME SAY THAT YOU AND YOUR PEOPLE, EVEN IF YOU WERE SINCERE, COULDN'T ERASE THE ACCUMULATED SUFFERING OF 200 YEARS.

FOR THIS REASON I CANNOT CALL YOU MY BROTHER!

CLAP CLAP CLAP CLAP CLAP
CLAP CLAP CLAP CLAP CLAP
CLAP CLAP CLAP CLAP
CLAP CLAP CLAP CLAP
CLAP CLAP CLAP
CLAP CLAP CLAP CLAP CLAP
CLAP CLAP CLAP CLAP CLAP
CLAP CLAP CLAP CLAP CLAP
CLAP CLAP CLAP CLAP CLAP
CLAP CLAP CLAP CLAP
CLAP CLAP
CLAP CLAP
CL

LIKE I SAID, YOUR TOKEN OFFERINGS OF SYMPATHY ARE PATRONIZING AND UNACCEPTABLE TO ME AND MY...

AMEN! PREACH IT!

WHEEE!

BUY BROTHER BIDDLE

"Hi there, young'uns. I'm **Naomi Muffin** of the LADIES BiBLE CLASS at First Church. Seems we gals have grown out of our old classroom facilities and are looking to cop a little positive cashflow. We're sick of bake sales; that's why we're getting into MAIL ORDER MERCHANDISING!

The **Brother Biddle**® Collection

"Remember your leaders
who spoke the word of God to you."
HEBREWS 13:7

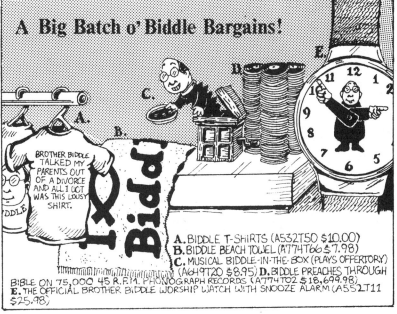

The Biddle Phone

NEED THAT EXTRA PUSH TO GET ON THE HORN AND MAKE THOSE BLASTED CHURCH CALLS? HERE'S **BIDDLE** TO HAND YOU THE RECEIVER AND WATCH PATIENTLY WHILE YOU GET IT DONE. NEED STRENGTH TO RESIST GOSSIPING ABOUT CHURCH FRIENDS? HERE'S **BIDDLE** TO KEEP AN EYE ON YOU! A PERFECT COMPANION FOR DIAL-A-PRAYER OR JUST ORDERING UP A LATE NIGHT PIZZA.

Biddle Phone
A694T26.........$49.98

Stuffed Biddle...He Talks!

LET'S TURN TOGETHER TO LEVITICUS!

BORED WITH LIFELESS SERMONS-ON-CASSETTE? NEVER AGAIN! NOW YOU CAN POP BIDDLE'S LATEST SERMON INTO THIS CUTE, HUGGABLE CLERGYMAN AND HE WILL **SEEM TO PREACH!** HE'S YOUR PLUSH PILLOW PASTOR ALWAYS THERE WITH A WARM, THEOLOGICALLY SOUND SMILE.

ALSO MAKES A GREAT PORTABLE RADIO FOR EXCITING SPORTING EVENTS.

Plush Biddle w/AM/FM/Cass.
A756T39.................$98.98

HOLY HOMILETICS... IT'S THE BIDDLE SIGNAL!

CONTROVERSY RAGES: YOU AND A FRIEND CANNOT AGREE ON THE IDENTITY OF THE **TRUE** AUTHOR OF "HEBREWS." NOT TO WORRY! JUST PLUG IN **THE BIDDLE SIGNAL** AND THE COLLARED CRUSADER WILL RUSH TO YOUR AID!
A630T56............$137.50

The **Brother Biddle**® Collection

ORDER FORM

℅ THE LADIES BIBLE CLASS 1224 GREENFIELD DRIVE EL CAJON CAL 92021 · WE ACCEPT FOOD STAMPS

NAME_____ ADDRESS_____ CITY_____ STATE___ ZIP___

QTY	DESCRIPTION	ITEM #	TOTAL BUCKS
	GRAND TOTAL BIG BUCKS		

BROTHER BIDDLE® AND THE REST OF HIS FAMILY ARE THE SOLE PROPERTY OF FIRST CHURCH. ANY EXPLOITATION ATTEMPTS OTHER THAN THOSE OF FIRST CHURCH AND NAOMI MUFFIN ARE STRICTLY PROHIBITED. SO THERE.

INTERESTED IN SELLING OUR PRODUCTS TO YOUR FRIENDS? ASK ABOUT BIDWAY!

AND PLEASE...DON'T MENTION ANYTHING ABOUT THIS TO BROTHER BIDDLE. THANK YOU.

Brother Biddle

FIRST CHURCH
SUNDAY: OUR PASTOR'S HOT NEW VIDEO

By Rob Suggs

"BIDDLE"... TUNE OF "BEAT IT." TAKE ONE!

"BIDEO" TAKE 1

YOUR MAMA RAISED YOU UP TO BE A FINE GUY... SHE TOLD YOU, "GO TO CHURCH, DON'T ASK ME WHY."... SO YOU SIT ON MY PEWS AND YOU YAWN AND YOU SIGH, "OLD BIDDLE..."

I PREACH MY HEART OUT AND I GIVE YOU MY ALL...YOU'D RATHER BE OUT AT THE SHOPPING MALL...YOU THINK ABOUT IT DURING MY ALTAR CALL, NOT BIDDLE... NOT BIDDLE!

I'M BIDDLE, BIDDLE, BIDDLE, I KEEP MY SERMONS IN THE MIDDLE; NEVER TOO FUNKY - ALWAYS UPRIGHT - IT DOESN'T MATTER, JUST SO I'M WHITE... I'M BIDDLE ...   I'M BIDDLE!!

I PASS THE PLATE AROUND, WE PLAY A SOFT HYMN... I ASK YOU LET'S GET DOWN LET'S BUILD A GYM... BUT WITH YOUR OFFERING OUR CHANCES LOOK SLIM, FOR BIDDLE.. FOR BIDDLE...

THE DEACONS HAVE A MEETING ONLY TO FUSS..."YOU HOLD THE BUDGET DOWN, SUBMIT TO US.". SO I DRIVE TO WORK IN AN ANCIENT CHURCH BUS, POOR BIDDLE...POOR BIDDLE!

BROTHER BIDDLE
HEAVEN METAL
BY ROB SUGGS

SON, WHAT WE NEED IS A **YOUTH OUTING!** A REALLY **SWELL** ONE!

AW, DAD... HAYRIDES AND STUFF ARE SO...

SQUARE? HEY, I CAN **DIG** IT... WELL, WHAT **DO** KIDS GO TO TODAY?

LET'S DO IT!

WELL, **ROCK** CONCERTS, BUT...

DAD, I **REALLY** DON'T THINK...

COME ON, SON, DON'T BE A **WIMP.' JESUS** ALLWAYS WENT WHERE THE **ACTION** WAS!

SURE THING, FOLKS! WE'LL HAVE TIMMY AND PUNKIN BACK BY ELEVEN!

WHAT'S "BOOGIE-'TIL-THE-COWS-COME-HOME," BROTHER BIDDLE?

I'M **NOT** BROTHER BIDDLE. COOL IT, TIMMY.

BORN TO ROCK 'N' ROLL

POP... THE KIDS SAY THEY DON'T WANT TO HEAR YOUR SERMON TAPES, HERE'S A CASSETTE OF THE GROUP WE'RE GOING TO HEAR!

(CLICK)

IT'S LOVE LEPROSY, YA GOT MY SKIN A'CRAWLIN'...

CHURCH BUS

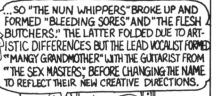

... SO "THE NUN WHIPPERS" BROKE UP AND FORMED "BLEEDING SORES" AND "THE FLESH BUTCHERS." THE LATTER FOLDED DUE TO ARTISTIC DIFFERENCES BUT THE LEAD VOCALIST FORMED "MANGY GRANDMOTHER" WITH THE GUITARIST FROM "THE SEX MASTERS," BEFORE CHANGING THE NAME TO REFLECT THEIR NEW CREATIVE DIRECTIONS.

SO WHAT DO THEY CALL THEMSELVES NOW?

"AXE WIELDING BLOOD SUCKING SPACE MUTANTS."

GREAT...

AT PRECISELY **11:37** AM EVERY SUNDAY **THE SUN'S RAYS** ENTER A FIRST CHURCH STAINED GLASS WINDOW AT SUCH AN ANGLE THAT **CHOIR MEMBERS MUST AVERT THEIR EYES FROM THE GREENISH GLARE REFLECTING OFF BIDDLE'S HEAD!** BIDDLE USUALLY READS A PASSAGE FROM **REVELATION** AT THIS POINT.

BROTHER BIDDLE USES **LOUD ANTHEMS** FOR SNEEZING, THROAT-CLEARING, BELCHING AND HICCUPING; **PRAYERS** FOR ZIPPER-CHECKING, NOSE-WIPING, AND GUM-CHANGING, AND **GUEST-PREACHERS** FOR DOING HIS TAXES!

FIRST CHURCH ATTENDANCE ROSE **76%** WHEN BIDDLE BEGAN SUBSTITUTING **CHICKEN NUGGETS** FOR THE COMMUNION WAFERS!

BROTHER BIDDLE ONCE PREACHED A 12-WEEK SERMON SERIES ON THE FACT THAT THE BOOK OF **NAHUM** SPELLS "**HUMAN**" **BACKWARDS**...BEFORE DISCOVERING IT **DOESN'T!**

NAHUM
MUHAN

IF ALL OF **BROTHER BIDDLE'S** CLERICAL COLLARS WERE LAID END-TO-END THEY WOULD **COVER THE EARTH,** CAUSING 7 YEARS OF **DARKNESS!** AS A MATTER OF FACT, BIBLICAL PROPHECY SEEMS TO **PREDICT SUCH AN EVENT!**

that's INCREDIBIDDLE!

FIRST CHURCH STARTED THE **LEISURE SUITS FOR AFRICA** MOVEMENT NOW SWEEPING ELDERLY CHURCH GROUPS ALL OVER THE NATION!

FEW LAYMEN REALIZE PASTORS KEEP **STATS.** "BATTING AVERAGE," FOR INSTANCE, IS THE RATIO OF WEDDINGS PERFORMED TO DIVORCES. "**R.B.I.'s**" ARE THE RESULTING **BAPTIZABLE INFANTS** AND A "**HOMER**" IS A TITHER MARRIED INTO THE CHURCH; AND IF HE THEN PUTS THE CHURCH IN HIS **WILL,** THEN BY GOLLY IT'S A "**GRAND SLAM.**"

Brother Biddle
LOOKS BACK!

IT IS A TIME FOR MEMORIES. AS A FIT OF NOSTALGIA OVERWHELMS OUR HERO, SPIRITS FROM THE PAST RISE FORTH TO BREAK DANCE THROUGH THE GHETTOS OF HIS MIND. THE MAN RECOGNIZES THESE SPECTRAL FIGURES. HE RISES TO GRAPPLE WITH THEM ANEW, AND HE RESPONDS THE ONE WAY HE KNOWS HOW: HE NODS OFF.

Z

ALBUM

ALMOST FROM THE BEGINNING, YOUNG BIDDLE SEEMED A CHILD OF DESTINY.

MR. BIDDLE, YOU'RE THE FATHER OF A **BOUNCING BABY REVEREND!**

WHAT DENOMINATION?

SHUNNING THE PLAYTHINGS OF ANY AVERAGE INFANT, HE WAS ATTRACTED TO HIGHER REALITIES.

SON
FATHER
HOLY GHOST

OTHERS RECOGNIZED IN HIM AN INTENSE SPIRITUALITY, AND IN TIME HIS REPUTATION BEGAN TO SPREAD.

BILLY, BE MINDFUL OF YOUR ACTIONS! IS IT NOT BETTER TO BE WITHOUT ALL WORLDLY GIFTS THAN TO OFFEND A LOWLY BROTHER? GIVE BIFF YOUR FROGGY!

OKAY.

I ♥ LIMITED ATONEMENT

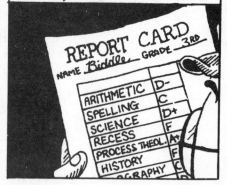

HIS SPECIAL TALENTS SHONE LIKE A BEACON, AS DID HIS DEFICIENCIES.

REPORT CARD
NAME Biddle GRADE 3RD

ARITHMETIC	D-
SPELLING	C
SCIENCE	D+
RECESS	F
PROCESS THEOL.	A+
HISTORY	F
GEOGRAPHY	C

ADOLESCENCE BROUGHT ITS TIMES OF TURBULENCE. NOT EVERYONE UNDERSTOOD HIM.

AH, GLORIA, WE'RE OUT OF GAS -- BUT THE MOON IS FULL... WOULD YOU LIKE TO DISCUSS HERMENEUTICS?

sigh.

THE TIME CAME TO EMBRACE DESTINY.

MY PLACEMENT SCORES? DON'T TELL ME... FIREMAN? NAH, THAT'S NOT IT... STOCK CAR RACER? NO? HOW ABOUT PRO WRESTLER?

GUIDANCE COUNSELOR

AS FATE WOULD HAVE IT, HE FOUND THAT SPECIAL OTHER... A KINDRED HEART... ONE MEANT FOR HIM SINCE TIME BEGAN.

YOU'VE HEARD OF ST. PAUL? THIS IS AMAZING! HE HAPPENS TO BE MY FAVORITE!

DIDN'T HE SLAY A DRAGON?

IT WAS HER STRENGTH, HER RESOURCEFUL-NESS THAT PULLED HIM THROUGH SEMIN-ARY. SHE SCRIMPED, SCROUNGED WHAT FEW PENNIES WERE ATTAINABLE.

LOUIE...IT'S MRS. B...ODDS ARE 3-1 ON A $100 OFFERING TAKE AT FIRST CHURCH... 2-1 ON REV. BLATT FINISHING BEFORE NOON... LEFTY, WHAT'VE WE GOT ON THE YOUTH DIRECTOR LOTTERY?...

AFTER YEARS OF STUDY, THE CALL CAME. A CHURCH AWAITED. HE PREACHED HIS FIRST SERMON; THE RESPONSE WAS STRONG

"...How Jesus loves each grassy hill, each leafy tree, the daffodil...

BOOO!

HISSS HISSSS

THUNK!

GET TO THE POINT

Booo Boob

ACTUALLY, NONE OF THIS HAPPENED. PIZZA LUNCHES ALWAYS GIVE BIDDLE FUNKY DREAMS.

I HOPE IT'S NOT BLASPHEM-OUS TO USE BAPTISMAL WATER...

MRS. STRONG

BEFORE LONG PROTESTANT POR

Z

SUGGS

WHY IS IT, BROTHER BIDDLE, THAT ALL OF THE CHURCH'S EVENTS REVOLVE AROUND FOOD?

UM... BECAUSE OF THE SACRAMENTAL EFFECT OF SHARING A MEAL TO ENHANCE FELLOWSHIP?

GREAT PASTA, MRS. TORTELLINI!

WELL... BUT WE DENOUNCE DRUG AND ALCOHOL ABUSE WHILE SPONSORING CALORIC ORGIES.

HAVE YOU TRIED AGNES LIMBERGER'S SOUFFLÉ? IT'S DOWNRIGHT SINFUL!

THAT'S **JUST** THE POINT! ISN'T **GLUTTONY** EVERY BIT AS SINFUL AS... AS... SAY, ARE THOSE CANDIED KUMQUATS?

YOU'VE NEVER TRIED MISS NAOMI'S KUMQUATS? WHAT DOES YOUR CHURCH **DO** FOR COMMUNION?

HONEY, WHY IS IT THAT **EVERY** GATHERING OF CHURCH FOLK SEEMS TO INCLUDE FOOD AND EXCESSIVE GLUTTONY?

OH, DON'T BE OVERCRITICAL. THE **FEAST** IS AN IMPORTANT TRADITION OF ECCLESIASTICAL FELLOWSHIP.

PERHAPS; BUT TO ME, IT SEEMS **INSENSITIVE** WITH SO MANY PEOPLE **STARVING.**

WELL THEN, I **SUPPOSE** YOU'LL FIND **SOME** WAY TO CRITICIZE OUR UPCOMING "**WORLD HUNGER AWARENESS** BUILD-YOUR-OWN-BANANA-SPLIT BASH!"

Brother Biddle PRESENTS... "The Raven"

apologies to E.A. POE

ONCE UPON A MIDNIGHT DREARY, AS I PONDERED, WEAK AND WEARY, OVER MANY A SERMON TOPIC BOUND TO BORE...
WHILE I NODDED, NEARLY NAPPING, SUDDENLY THERE CAME A TAPPING, AS OF SOMEONE GENTLY RAPPING, RAPPING AT MY OFFICE DOOR.
SOME SILLY DEACON, NOTHING MORE.

AS I SAT AND THOUGHT IT OVER, THERE IN SUCH A BLEAK OCTOBER, FEELING PRETTY SAD AND SOBER, THROUGH MY PREACHING FILES I'D PORE.
SUMMER GONE, FOLKS WERE RETURNING TO THE PEWS FOR BIBLE LEARNING, WITH A QUITE ANNOYING YEARNING HARD FOR PASTORS TO IGNORE...
ENTERTAINMENT EVERMORE!

FASTER!

BUT THE SOUND I HEARD OF KNOCKING, AT MY DOOR TOO LATE FOR LOCKING, STILL WAS ROLLING AND WAS ROCKING; WHY ON EARTH THIS LATE UPROAR?
IN THERE FLEW A RAVEN STATELY, BLOWING ME AWAY QUITE GREATLY FOR I HADN'T SEEN ONE LATELY AT THE CHURCH I'M WORKING FOR.
BUT HE PERCHED AND NOTHING MORE.

INOFFENSIVE EXHORTATIONS FOR EVERY OCCASION

I RESUMED MY RESTLESS SQUIRMIN', SEARCHING FOR A WORTHY SERMON, SCANNING VOLUMES FRENCH AND GERMAN SPREAD UPON MY DESK AND FLOOR. "I GIVE UP!" I SOBBED, DEFEATED. "SURE, INSPIRED PREACHING'S NEEDED, BUT MY THEMES HAVE BEEN REPEATED 'TIL MY PEOPLE START TO SNORE." QUOTH THE RAVEN: "PREACH IT! MORE!"

GREAT, I THOUGHT, NOW BIRDS ARE FLOCKING TO MY STUDY JUST FOR MOCKING BIDDLE'S BURNOUT; TIME FOR LOCKING OLD FIRST CHURCH'S LOUSY DOOR. "WAIT A MINUTE!" CRIED THE BIRD. "I KNOW YOU THINK ME WEIRD, ABSURD, BUT HAS IT TO YOU YET OCCURRED, THAT I FOR ONE MAY KNOW THE SCORE? ... SERMONS FRESH FOR EVERMORE!"

I STOPPED TO LISTEN, QUITE DUMBFOUNDED. HE WAS RIGHT: **INSANE** IT SOUNDED; YET HIS WORDS SEEMED FIRMLY GROUNDED IN A TRUTH ONE CAN'T IGNORE. "WHAT YOU SAID, IN DESPERATE REACHING, FOR A LESSON WORTH THE TEACHING – **THAT**, MY FRIEND, IS CHRISTIAN PREACHING THAT YOUR FOLKS ARE SEARCHING FOR.   BE YOURSELF, AND NOTHING MORE!"

"THAT'S SIMPLISTIC," I PROTESTED. "TELEVISION'S JUST INFESTED WITH SLICK PREACHING; I'LL BE BESTED IF I'M JUST **MYSELF** (A BORE)."
    "HOGWASH! BULL!" THE BIRD DISPUTED. GOD HAS NEVER **YET** RECRUITED ONE TO BE A FANCY-SUITED SALESMAN FROM THE HOLY STORE...
            JUST YOURSELF AND NOTHING MORE."

"IF YOU'VE DRIED UP, NEVER HIDE IT. SIMPLY TRY TO CLIMB INSIDE IT; CHECK IT OUT AND THEN CONFIDE IT TO THE ONES YOU'RE PREACHING FOR. AUTHENTIC PREACHING REALLY DELVES NOT INTO BOOKS UPON THE SHELVES BUT INTO TRUTH INSIDE OURSELVES: IT'S AT THE VERY CORE.
    "PREACH THE TRUTH FOREVER MORE!"

THEN I ASKED HIM, QUITE GLAD-HEARTED, JUST BEFORE THE BIRD DEPARTED, HOW HE'D EVER GOTTEN STARTED, LEARNING PASTOR LORE.
    "IT'S A JOB," THE RAVEN STATED; "SOLD INSURANCE, WHICH I HATED. LOVE MY WORK, I WOULDN'T TRADE IT." THEN I WATCHED HIM SOAR. WHO KNOWS? MAYBE TO YOUR DOOR.

RING!

RING!
RING!
CLICK.

GRACE AND PEACE! BROTHER BIDDLE HERE; ACCEPT MY CONTRITE REPENTANCE FOR BEING ELSEWHERE AT YOUR TIME OF NEED. KNOW THAT, IF I WERE HOME TO TAKE YOUR CALL, OR IF INDEED YOUR TITHES AND OFFERINGS JUSTIFIED MY USE OF A CELLULAR CAR PHONE OR, FOR THAT MATTER, A CAR, I WOULD BE AT YOUR UNMITIGATED DISPOSAL.

IN ALL PROBABILITY, HOWEVER, I AM AT ANY OF THIRTY-SEVEN-ODD CHURCH COMMITTEE MEETINGS WHICH MANDATE MY INERRANT ATTENDANCE. EVEN NOW I MAY BE PARTAKING IN SPIRITED WRANGLING OVER CHANGING COMMUNION WAFER BRANDS...OR WHETHER TO REUPHOLSTER THE PEWS.

OR YOU MIGHT POSSIBLY FIND ME AT THE HOSPITAL MINISTERING TO THE SICK, LISTENING ATTENTIVELY TO THE LOW SPIRITS OF THE TIRED AND TROUBLED...MANY OF THEM FORGOTTEN BY THEIR OWN LOVED ONES.

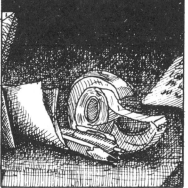

PERHAPS I AM NOW WITH YOUR CANCEROUS AUNT...OR THAT COUSIN TO WHOM YOU'VE BEEN MEANING TO SEND A BOUQUET. I'LL GIVE THEM YOUR LOVE... I ALWAYS DO.

BUT, OF COURSE, I MIGHT BE ELSEWHERE. I MIGHT BE WITH OL' POPS, WHO CALLS AT 4 A.M. IN AN ALCOHOLIC HAZE AND JUST NEEDS A FRIEND...

I MIGHT BE OUT MOWING THE CHURCH LAWN, SCRAPING GUM FROM THE PEWS, OR FIXING THE LEAK IN THE BAPTISMAL. **HOWEVER...**

IF I WEREN'T OCCUPIED IN ONE OF THE AFOREMENTIONED ENTERPRISES, YOU CAN BET YOUR BUDGET PLEDGE I WOULD, AS USUAL, SACRIFICE TIME WITH MY WIFE AND SON, OR PERHAPS SERMON PREPARATION, TO LISTEN TO YOUR COSMICALLY SIGNIFICANT CONCERNS.

AT THE SOUND OF THE TONE YOU WILL HEAR STRESS-REDUCING FLUTE MUSIC. SAY WHAT YOU LIKE. IT WILL NOT BE RECORDED, BUT YOU'LL FEEL BETTER. THIS IS YOUR PASTOR SAYING, "GO IN PEACE. *SELAH.*"

DON'T YOU THINK SOMEONE'S GOING TO NOTICE YOU NEVER ANSWER YOUR PHONE?

NOPE. THEY ONLY CALL ONCE.

Suggs 9/7/89

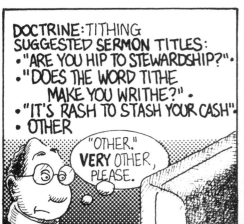

DOCTRINE: TITHING
SUGGESTED SERMON TITLES:
• "ARE YOU HIP TO STEWARDSHIP?" •
• "DOES THE WORD TITHE
     MAKE YOU WRITHE?" •
• "IT'S RASH TO STASH YOUR CASH"
• OTHER

"OTHER." **VERY** OTHER, PLEASE.

TARGETED LISTENER(S)
ENTER NAME(S):
  MISS NAOMI MUFFIN
  MR WINTHROP WADD
  MR. U.S. SIMOLEAN Ⅳ

I LIKE THIS FEATURE!

SEARCHING FILE
SEARCHING FILE
SEARCHING FILE
WARNING...N MUFFIN TARGETED
LISTENER 11 OF LAST 15 WEEKS
...SIMOLEAN QUOTE 8 FEB '87:
"I'M CHANGING DENOMINATIONS
NEXT TIME BIDDLE PREACHES ON
MONEY."...DELETE TARGETS?

NOPE! LET THE CHIPS FALL WHERE THEY MAY!

POWER PREACHING THE BIDDLE WAY

...AND GOD TOLD ME TO SAY THIS TO YOU, LEWIS, AND YOU, FRANCINE, IN TITUS WE FIND THAT...

HI, I'M **BROTHER BIDDLE**. A NEW SENSATION IS SWEEPING OUR NATION. THE '50'S GAVE US THE HULA HOOP. MINI-SKIRTS WERE ALL THE RAGE IN THE '60'S; DISCO HIT BIG IN THE '70'S WHILE AIRLINE DISASTERS WERE IN STYLE IN THE '80'S. BUT TODAY...EVERYONE'S PREACHING!

YES, PREACHING'S BEEN WITH US FOR A COUPLE MILLENNIA. BUT IN THE OLD DAYS, YOU HAD TO HAVE A TROUBLESOME **THEOLOGICAL FOUNDATION** FOR ANYONE TO LISTEN. BUT NOW, **EVERYONE'S** AN EXPERT! FROM PLAYGROUND PROPHETS IN NORTH CAROLINA, TO MOTIVATIONAL GURUS, THERE ARE MORE **PREACHERS** THAN **PEOPLE!**

SUCCE

THE DAYS OF BEING ANCHORED TO YOUR PULPIT ARE OVER. BODY LANGUAGE CAN SPEAK LOUDER THAN WORDS. TRY SOME OF THESE "THEOLOGICAL STANCES..."

FOR 994 MORE PREACHING POSITIONS, JUST WRITE FOR MY NEW VIDEO, "BODY BY BIDDLE."

NOTHING PUTS 'EM TO SLEEP AS FAST AS **DRY RHETORIC.** IF JESSE JACKSON TAUGHT US ANYTHING, IT'S THAT IT'S **SUBLIME** TO USE A **PRIME RHYME** EVERY **TIME!** PREACHING NEEDS TO **SOUND** GOOD.

WANT MORE? WRITE TODAY FOR **"HEY DIDDLE BIDDLE,"** MY NEW CASSETTE... OR BORROW SOME **DR. SEUSS** FROM YOUR KIDS.

AN IDLE CONGREGATION IS THE DEVIL'S PLAYGROUND... THAT'S WHY YOU'VE GOT TO GET **AUDIENCE PARTICIPATION** IN YOUR SERMON. TRY THESE TWO TECHNIQUES:

"LOONY LITURGY"

"STUMP THE CHOIR"

ALL THE GREAT PULPITEERS REMEMBER TO ADD A PINCH OF **SLOPPY SENTIMENT** TO THE RECIPE.
WE KEEP HANKIES BY THE HYMNALS IN **OUR** PEWS... HOW ABOUT **YOU?**

EXCUSE US, BUT WE SEE THE **BACK COVER** LOOMING AHEAD. IT LOOKS LIKE OUR BOOK HAS RUN OUT OF TIME, BROTHER B.

...AND WE WOULDN'T WANT TO MAKE EVERYBODY LATE TO THE CAFETERIA...

WHEATON EVANGELICAL WONDERLAND

DOWN GRAVE

CAROL STREAM

HEAVEN FORBID. WELL NOW... ARE YOU GOING TO GIVE AN INVITATION? WE'LL HUM "JUST AS I AM..."

WHY, **YES.** ALL OUR READERS ARE CORDIALLY INVITED TO **BIDDLE II: MISS NAOMI'S REVENGE!**

PUNCH LINES

HOT ECCLESIASTICAL TRENDS

TELEVANGELIST SHTICK

WE SUPPOSE IT WAS INEVITABLE. ANY FINAL WORDS AS WE PUT THIS BABY TO BED?

JUST THAT I'M **HONORED** TO HAVE DONE THIS GIG AND I HOPE I'VE LIVED UP TO THE **GREAT CARTOON EVANGELICALS** OF MY TRADITION.

UH, WE HATE TO BREAK IT TO YOU, BUT **YOU** ARE THE ONLY CARTOON EVAN--

OH... **CALVINIST COW** AND **PENTECOSTAL PIG** ARE HERE FOR ME. I'M OUTA HERE.

HAPPY **THEOLOGICAL TRAILS,** YOU ALL!

SUGGS